MAPS

GETTING FROM
HERE TO THERE

HARVEY WEISS

Houghton Mifflin Company   Boston   1991

The author is indebted to the following organizations and
individuals who have assisted in the preparation of this book:
David Fox, David Rothenberg, Stanley Bleifeld, John Weiss, the
New York Public Library, the New York City Transportation
Authority, Jeppesen Sanderson, Inc., the United States Department
of the Interior–Geological Survey, the State of Florida
Transportation Department, and the United States Department
of Commerce–National Ocean Service.

Library of Congress Cataloging-in-Publication Data

Weiss, Harvey.
    Maps : getting from here to there / Harvey Weiss.
      p.   cm.
    Summary: Discusses various aspects of maps including direction,
distance, symbols, latitude, and longitude, how maps are made,
special purpose maps, and charts.
    ISBN 0-395-56264-3
    1. Maps — Juvenile literature. [1. Maps.] I. Title.
GA105.6.W45   1991
j 912 — dc20   90-25069
                       CIP
                       AC

Printed in the United States of America

HOR 10 9 8 7 6 5 4 3 2 1

CONTENTS

INTRODUCTION

Where am I?

Do you want to know where I am at
this very moment? and how to get
here from absolutely anywhere?
I'll tell you with the help of a few maps.

1. Here is a map of my desk, with me sitting at it.

2. Here is where the desk is in my room.

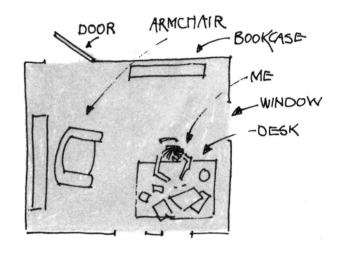

3. And this is where the room is in my house.

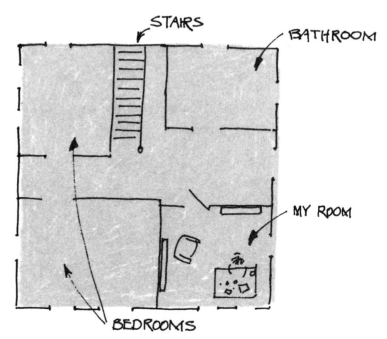

4. Here is where my house is located in my town. (My town is fairly large, so instead of showing you the entire town on this map, I will just show you the neighborhood where I live.)

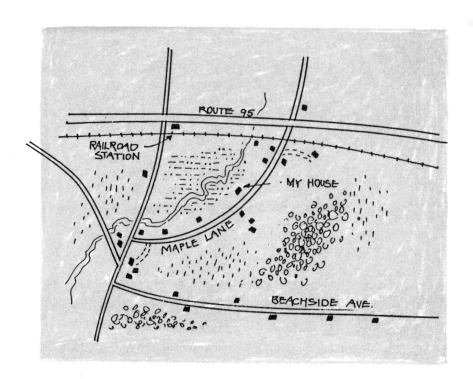

5. I live in the state of Connecticut, and my town is shown on this map of the state.

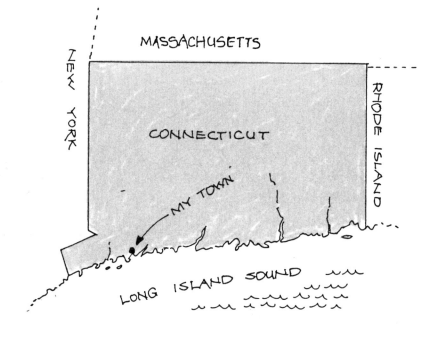

6. Connecticut is on this map
of the United States.

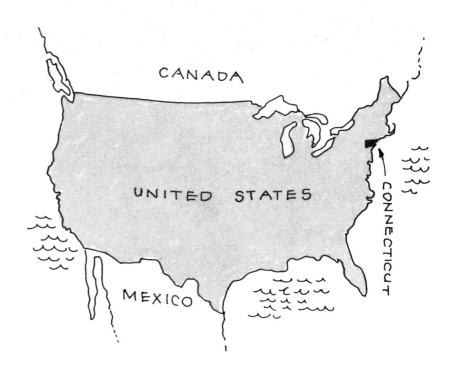

7. And the United States is shown on
this map of the entire world.

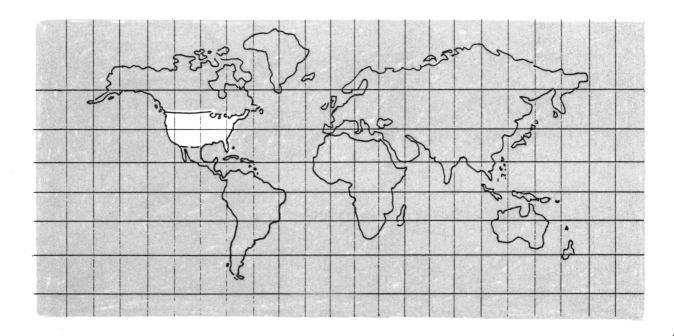

8. If you were a traveler arriving
from outer space and wanted to find me,
you would need a map to locate the
planet Earth. And then, by retracing
the preceding steps, you would end up at
my desk and have a visit with me!

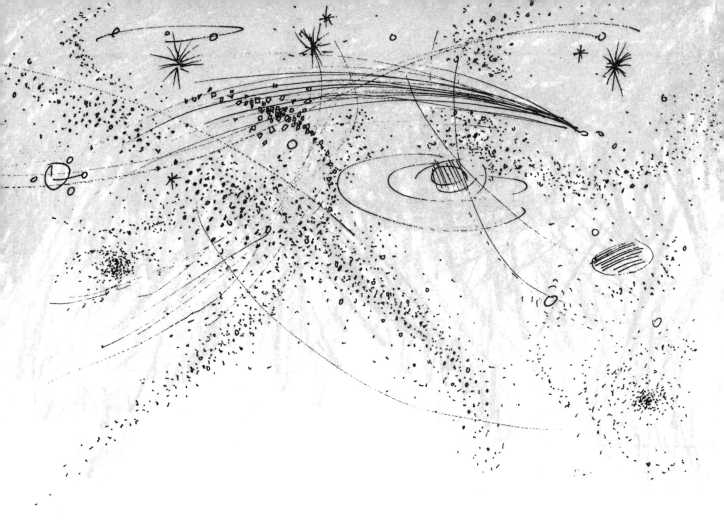

A map is like a diagram, a sort of blueprint that can give
you a great deal of information about many things. The study
of geography would be very difficult if there were no maps to
refer to. Maps tell you about the surface of the earth — the
land and sea, and the animal and plant life on it. There are
maps of the moon, too, and maps of the land under the
oceans — maps of almost anything you can think of.

Maps are important for anyone who is traveling or
backpacking or exploring — or just plain curious and eager to
learn about the world we live in. Maps are essential if you
don't want to get lost in strange places, and they are great fun
to use if you know how.

1.
WHICH WAY?

One of the most important things a map can do is help you
get where you want to go. In order to do that, it must show you
direction. If you want to get somewhere, you must know in
what direction the place is.

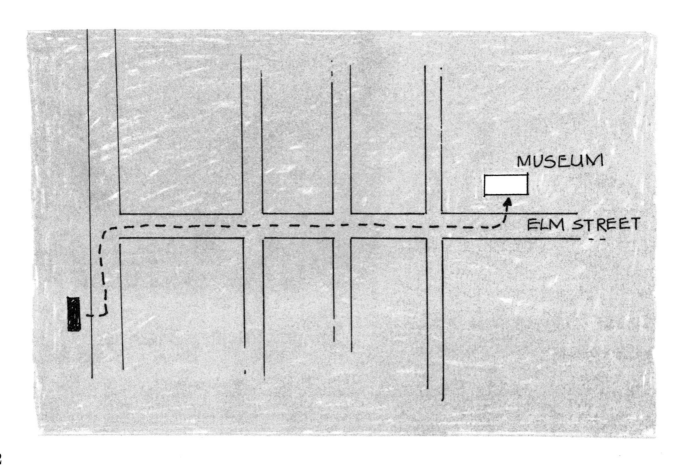

Let's suppose you were visiting a friend in a strange city and decided to go to the art museum by yourself. If you had a map like the one shown on the opposite page, you would be able to find it with no trouble. Just walk out the door, turn left, then right onto Elm Street. Walk three blocks and there is the art museum on your left. Very simple!

But what would you do if the museum and your friend's house were in a forest with no streets? You would have to know in what direction to walk. The map below tells us that the direction from the house to the museum is due east. We know this because directions are shown by the compass rose in the upper corner of the map. It shows which way is north, south, east, and west.

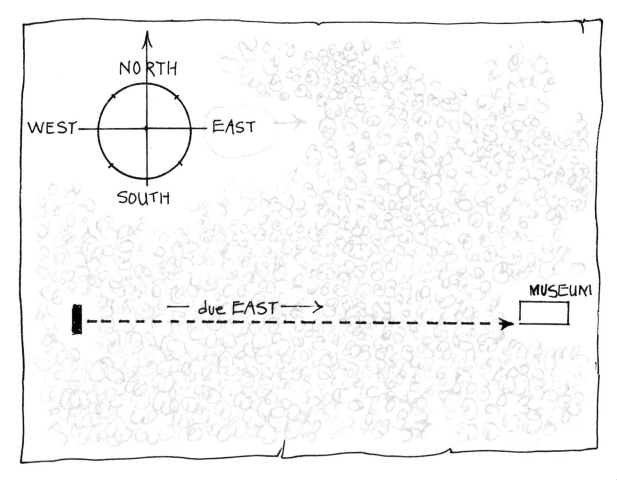

But, standing next to your friend's house, how do you tell which way is east? If it is early morning, you can tell. The sun comes up in the east, so all you have to do is walk in the direction of the rising sun, and sooner or later you will bump into the museum.

However, a much more dependable way to tell direction is with a compass. The needle of a compass always points north. Look at the face of the compass and notice which way is east, then head that way.

The dial, or face, of the compass will show north, east, south, and west, and it will also show degrees. All compass faces are divided into 360 equal parts, called degrees. East is 90 degrees, south is 180, west is 270, and north is 0 or 360 degrees. Using degrees is a simple and accurate way to tell direction.

A small inexpensive compass will often show only North, East, South, and West on its face. But it is much better when a compass also shows degrees.

How come the needle of a compass is so smart? How does it know which way is north? It knows because the compass needle is a small magnet. And the earth itself is also a magnet. The compass needle is attracted to the earth's north magnetic pole. It will always point north.

The smaller compasses have a needle that turns to point north. Large compasses have no needle. The face of the compass turns to show north.

You can make a compass yourself by rubbing a needle on a magnet. A big, hefty needle will work much better than a small, delicate one. Stroke the needle along the magnet a dozen or so times, moving it in the same direction each time. Then test it by seeing if it will pick up a pin or a paper clip.

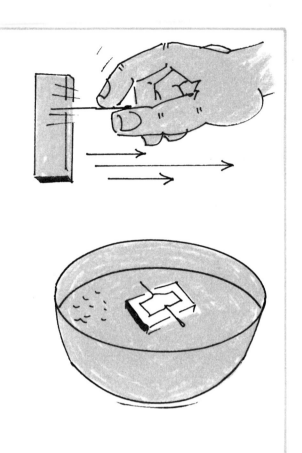

Tape the needle to a small piece of cork or plastic foam or wood and put it in a large bowl of water. Don't use a steel or iron bowl. Sometimes the blunt end of the needle will point north. This is because of the way you magnetized the needle. You can check your homemade compass against a regular one, if you have one, to see how accurate it is.

In modern aircraft and oceangoing vessels there are complicated devices that do the job of the compass. Satellites and computer navigation aids can tell you where you are and where you are heading at any moment. But the compass is still the most dependable, easy-to-use, best friend of the explorer, hiker, or anybody trying to find his or her way around in an unfamiliar place.

2.

HOW FAR?

The map on page 12 told you what streets to take in order to get to the art museum. The next map, on page 13, showed what direction to take since there are no streets to follow. The sun or a compass served as a guide. But there is something else you will want to know in addition to direction. That is how far to go.

If you want to get from one place to another on a map, you will want to know if your destination is nearby or far away. You have to know about distance.

At the bottom of most maps you will see what looks like a ruler. It shows the scale of the map. In fact, it is referred to as the "scale." It tells you about distances. The scale shown here is 1 inch equals 10 miles. This means that 1 inch on the map represents 10 miles on the ground. (Most maps show scale in both miles and kilometers.)

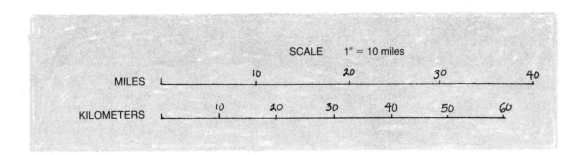

On the map shown here, the scale is 1 inch equals 1 mile. If you lay a ruler down on this map and measure the distance from Mount Kazooly to Lake Porgy, you will see that it is 6 inches. So you know that these two places are 6 miles apart.

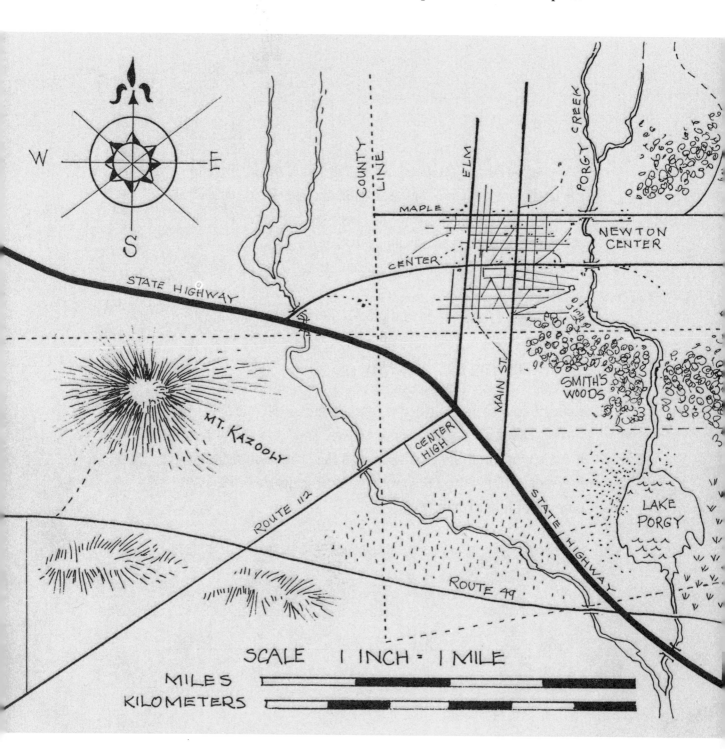

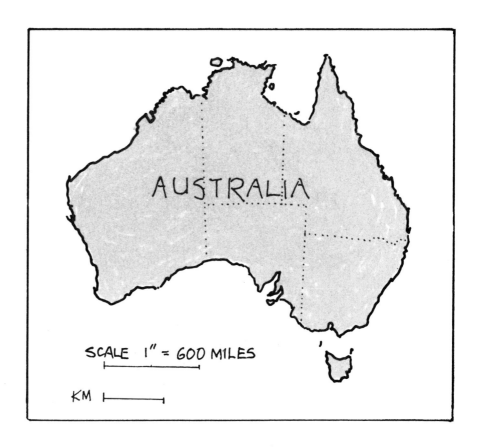

SCALE 1" = 600 MILES

KM

The scale is different on different maps. If the map shows a large area, like all of Australia, for example, the scale might be something like 1 inch equals 600 miles.

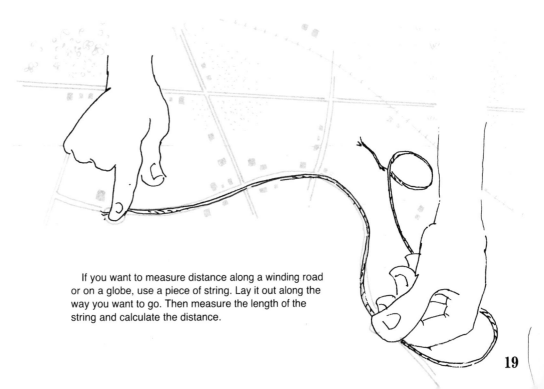

If you want to measure distance along a winding road or on a globe, use a piece of string. Lay it out along the way you want to go. Then measure the length of the string and calculate the distance.

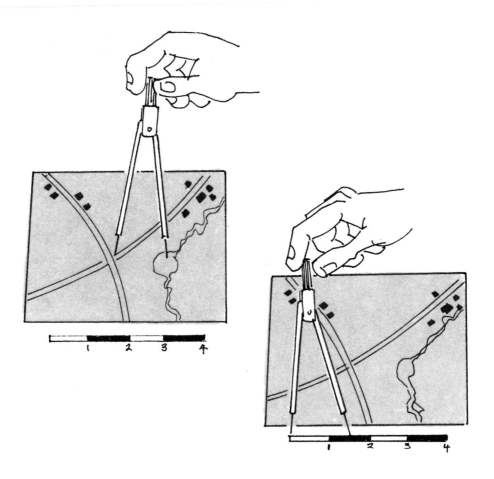

A pair of dividers is a useful tool for measuring distance. Place the points of the dividers on the two points you want to measure. Then move the dividers to the scale and figure the distance.

Scale is often given as a ratio, like this — 1:1,000. This means that what measures one space on a map is actually 1,000 spaces. Or, to put it another way, 1 inch on the map is 1,000 inches on the surface of the earth.

A map with a scale of 1:5,000 is a very large-scale map. It shows a close-up view of things, in great detail. A map with a scale of 1:50,000 would show a larger area, such as an entire city. A small-scale map showing all of Africa on one page would have a scale of something like 1:40,000,000. That means 1 inch equals 630 miles.

3.
WHAT'S THERE?

Maps can tell you many different things. But you must have the right map for what you want to know. If, for example, you wanted to know where in the United States Georgia is located, you would need a map of the entire country with all the states marked on it. It wouldn't help to have a map that showed only the heights of mountains, or where the population was most concentrated.

There are maps with all kinds of information. Some maps are made to show roads, mineral deposits, federal parks, camping sites, farm lands, and other special subjects. Maps that show states, districts, countries, and their capitals and borders, are called political maps.

This map covers the western part of the United States — the section west of the Mississippi River. It is a political map and shows only the location of the various states that are in this area.

Many maps have a key, or "legend," that will help you read it. The legend explains what the map is all about — what it is trying to tell you. The scale of the map is also given, of course, and there is often a compass rose or some other means of showing which way is north.

POPULATION

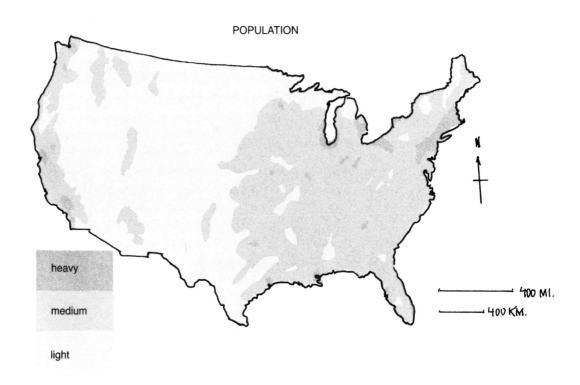

This map shows where people live in the United States. The light tan is where very few people live. The dark tan is where the most people live — where the population is heaviest — in the northeast and around Chicago, Detroit, parts of Florida, California, and a few other spots. The medium-tan area is for average population density.

Large-scale maps, or local maps — ones that take a close-up view — use symbols to give detailed information. Here are some of the more common ones:

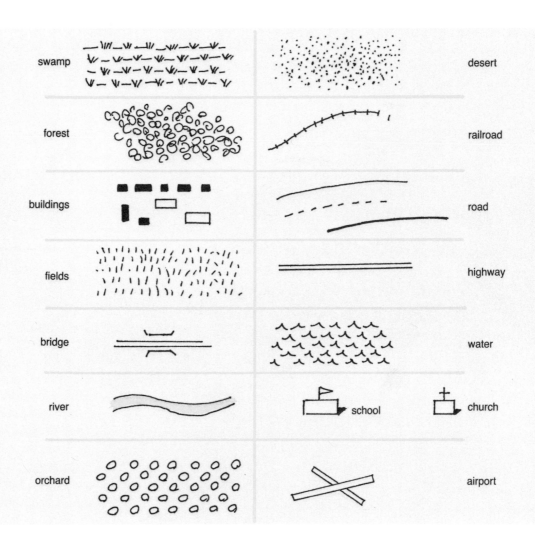

Although not shown here, color can give us much information when used on a map. Blue is usually used to show water. Different countries are sometimes shown in different colors, and the nature of the earth's surface can be suggested by the use of color.

Maps are important when you study geography and have to know what is happening on the surface of the earth. They can show how the forces of nature will affect life for many people. For example, the map below, showing the average rainfall in parts of North Africa, explains why there are vast deserts like the Sahara. And if there is sand and only a little water, we can understand why the people live in tents, travel by camel, and don't do any farming.

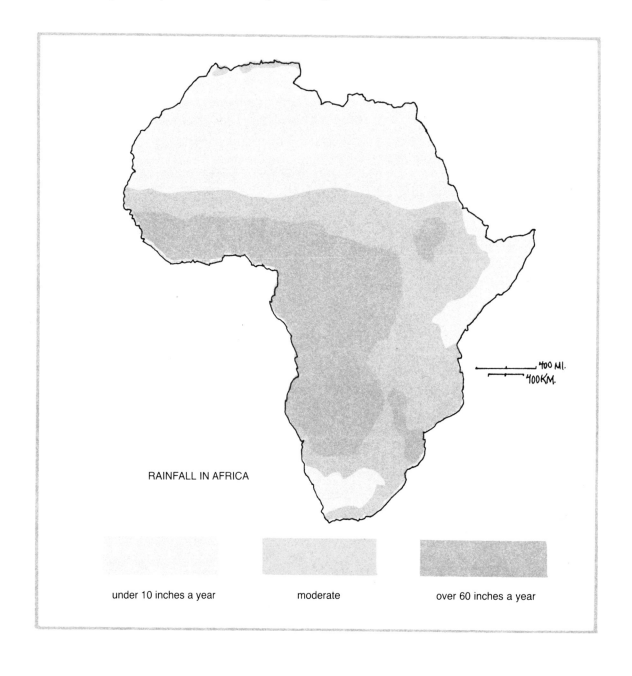

RAINFALL IN AFRICA

400 MI.
400 KM.

under 10 inches a year   moderate   over 60 inches a year

The Gulf Stream

North Pacific

North Atlantic

South Pacific

South Atlantic

Indian Ocean

Here is a different kind of map — one that shows ocean currents. The kind of information contained here is of great importance for boats traveling long distances, for fishermen, and for scientists concerned with weather and temperature and undersea life.

If you were planning a voyage by boat from Cuba to Spain, for example, you would want to study a map like this. You would probably decide not to head in a straight line between these two places. Rather, you might choose a more northerly, roundabout route that would take advantage of the Gulf Stream. This current, which is shown on this map, moves at approximately 6 miles per hour, and if you were on a small boat, it would save you time even if the distance traveled was greater.

A map like the one below is part map, part picture, and is mighty useful when traveling about in strange towns or cities. The one shown here is part of a large map that covers most of the city of Washington, D.C. With something like this in hand, you would not have much trouble locating the places you wanted to visit — museums, parks, government buildings. This kind of map is like a view from a slow-moving, low-flying airplane, but better. The view is very clear, places are easy to identify, and many streets and places are labeled!

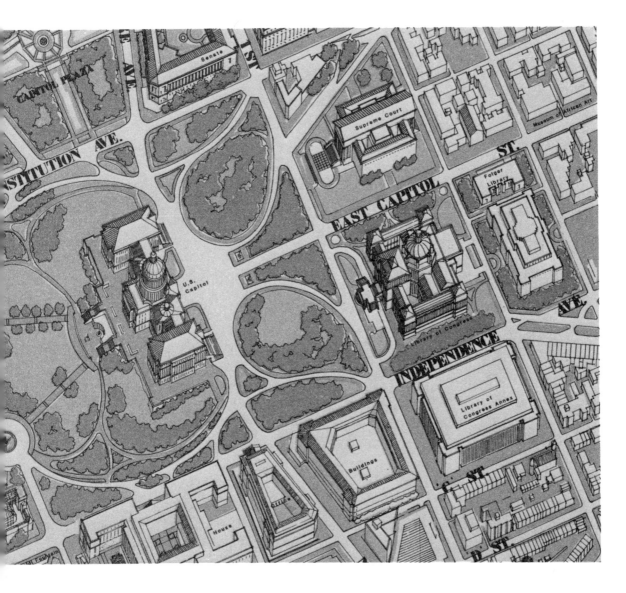

4.

UP AND DOWN

Very often it is important to know how high or low a place is. Suppose you were planning a bike trip. If the map showed a lot of steep hills along the route you were thinking of taking, you would probably decide to go somewhere else. Or suppose you were a road builder planning a highway from Switzerland to the Mediterranean Sea. What would be the best route? A map that showed mountains, cliffs, and valleys would be what you'd need. Then you could plan a road as level as possible.

Several different types of maps will give you this kind of information. One is a picture map, like the one on the next page. The use of shadows and realistic drawing gives a clear idea of where the hills and valleys are located and what they look like. This is an elevated view — looking down from above, not unlike the city map of Washington.

But the most useful map is a topographic map like the one on the facing page. A topographic map provides a most accurate description of the natural and manmade features on the surface of the earth. A topographic map shows elevation — the ups and downs — as well as such things as roads and lakes, cities and towns. A large-scale (close-up) topographic map will even show individual buildings. Maps of this sort are to be found in the pockets of most hikers and back-packers.

Elevations on a topographic map are shown by means of contour lines. Contour lines are like slices of the earth. The position of each slice is shown by a line. Each line is exactly the same distance above sea level. It is as if the entire earth were flooded, and as the water went down it left a mark every ten feet or so, like the rings in a bathtub. Little numbers on the contour lines tell you the elevation — just how high above sea level each line is.

It is easy to tell a steep slope from a flat place or a gentle slope by the placing of the lines. When the lines are close together the slope is steep. When the lines are far apart the land is flat. (In the case of a vertical cliff the lines would be one on top of the other!)

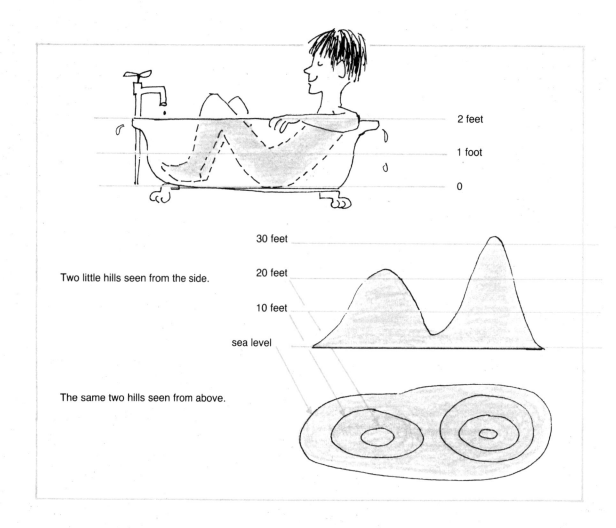

2 feet

1 foot

0

30 feet

20 feet

Two little hills seen from the side.

10 feet

sea level

The same two hills seen from above.

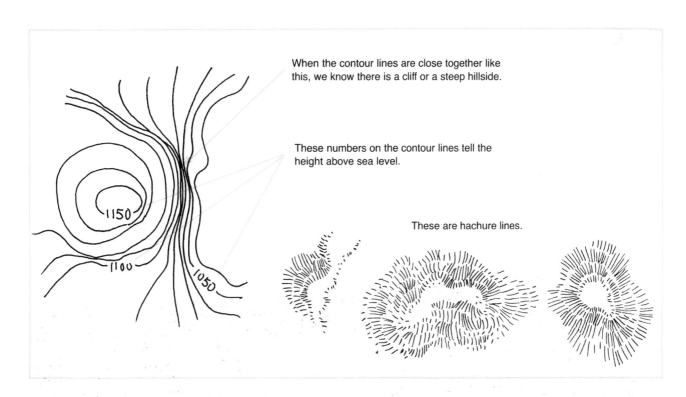

When the contour lines are close together like this, we know there is a cliff or a steep hillside.

These numbers on the contour lines tell the height above sea level.

These are hachure lines.

Sometimes short, straight lines are used to show mountains and valleys. The shorter and closer the lines, the steeper the slope. These lines are called hachure lines and give only an approximate idea of elevation. Still another way of showing elevation is with color. Brown is used for mountains, hills are in lighter shades of brown, and plains and lowlands are yellow and green. Water is always blue.

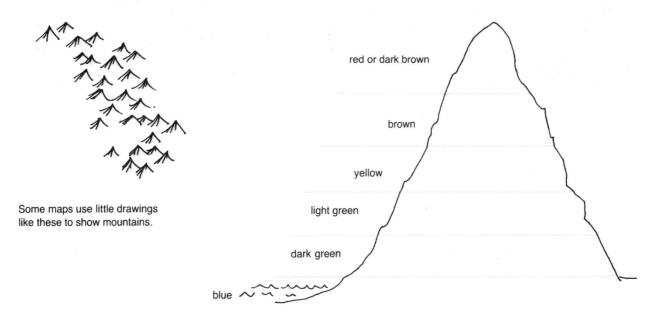

Some maps use little drawings like these to show mountains.

red or dark brown

brown

yellow

light green

dark green

blue

Explorers and travelers many centuries ago who didn't have the knowledge and skill to make accurate maps drew pictures, and these served to tell about places they visited. This "map" is a wood engraving from a travel book printed in the fifteenth century. A map like this might not get you exactly where you wanted to go, but it would at least give you some idea of what the town looked like!

5.
ALL THOSE LINES

Most maps will have lines running up and down (vertically) and from side to side (horizontally). The horizontal lines are called latitudes, and the vertical lines are called longitudes. The purpose of these lines is to help locate places on the surface of the earth.

The line that runs around the middle of the earth is called the equator, and all the latitudes are parallel to it. They are measured in degrees. The equator is 0 degrees. The next line up, shown on the globe on the next page, is 10 degrees north. The one above that is 20 degrees north, and so on all the way up to the North Pole, which is the very top of the earth and is 90 degrees north.

The lines of latitude that go down from the equator are also numbered from 0 to 90, but they are marked *south:* 10 degrees south, 20 degrees south, and so on.

A small circle (°) used next to a number means degrees. So, 20 degrees north is written 20° N.

The vertical, or longitude, lines run between the North Pole and the South Pole. They are divided into east and west longitudes. The line that separates the east lines of longitude from the west lines of longitude is a made-up, arbitrary line that runs through an observatory in Greenwich, England. This line is called the Greenwich meridian.

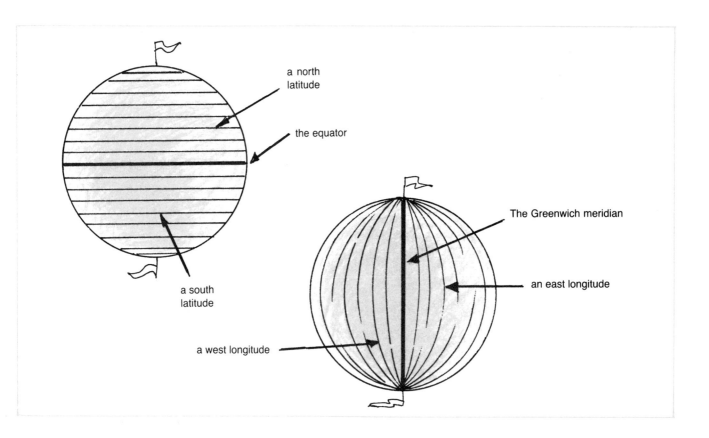

a north latitude

the equator

The Greenwich meridian

an east longitude

a south latitude

a west longitude

It is important to know if a line of longitude is east or west of the Greenwich meridian. For example, suppose you were trying to find Tokyo on a map of the world, and were told it was on the 140° line of longitude. If you looked for 140° west you would be looking for Tokyo in Alaska somewhere. You would be much better off looking along the line of 140° east — which goes through Japan!

Of course, to locate Tokyo accurately you would want to know how far up or down it was along this line of 140° east, and that would mean knowing its latitude.

Locating something by degrees of latitude and longitude is not accurate enough for most purposes. So each degree is broken down into 60 parts, called minutes. (This kind of minute is a measure of distance, not time!) And, sometimes, if you have to be extremely accurate, you can break the minutes down into seconds.

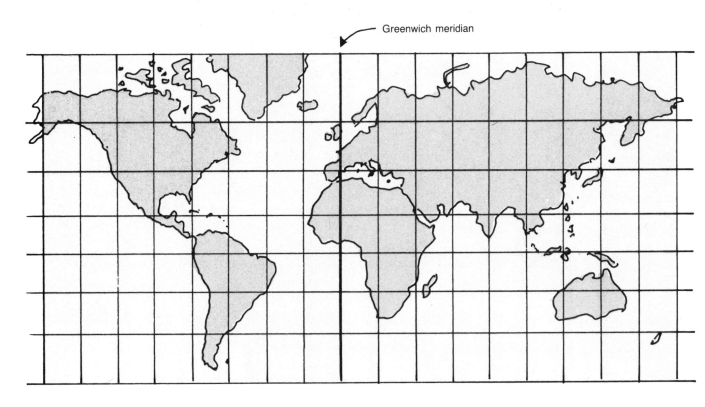

Greenwich meridian

The lines of latitude and longitude are shown as straight lines here. But on a small-scale map — one that shows big areas — you will often find these lines leaning at odd angles or curved. That is because of mapmakers' efforts to draw the surface of a sphere on a flat sheet of paper. The chapter on mapmaking describes some of the ways this is done.

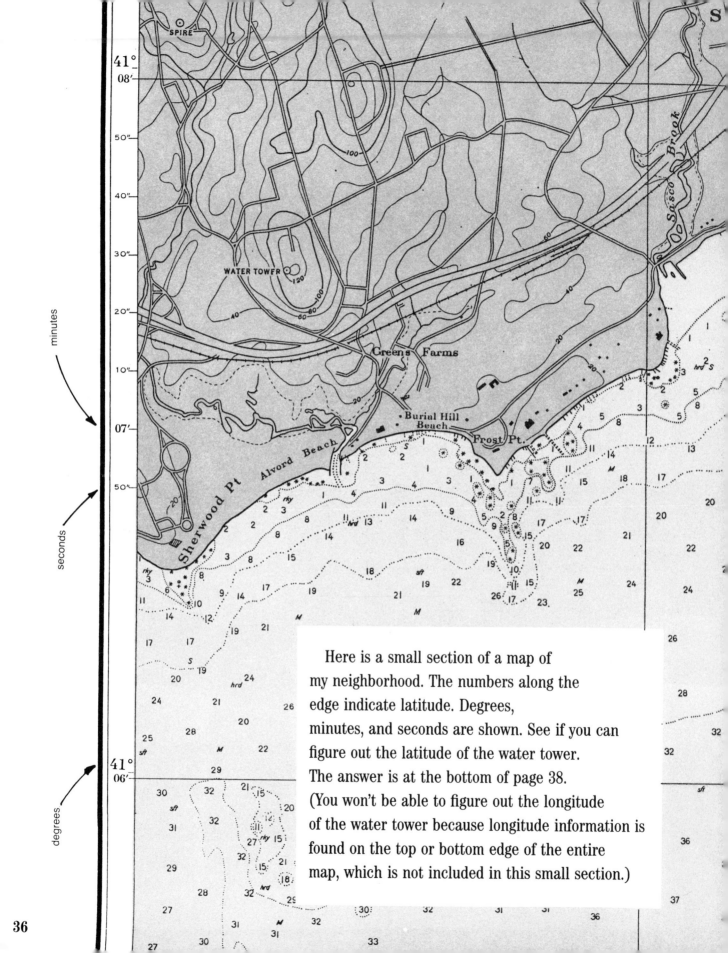

Here is a small section of a map of my neighborhood. The numbers along the edge indicate latitude. Degrees, minutes, and seconds are shown. See if you can figure out the latitude of the water tower. The answer is at the bottom of page 38. (You won't be able to figure out the longitude of the water tower because longitude information is found on the top or bottom edge of the entire map, which is not included in this small section.)

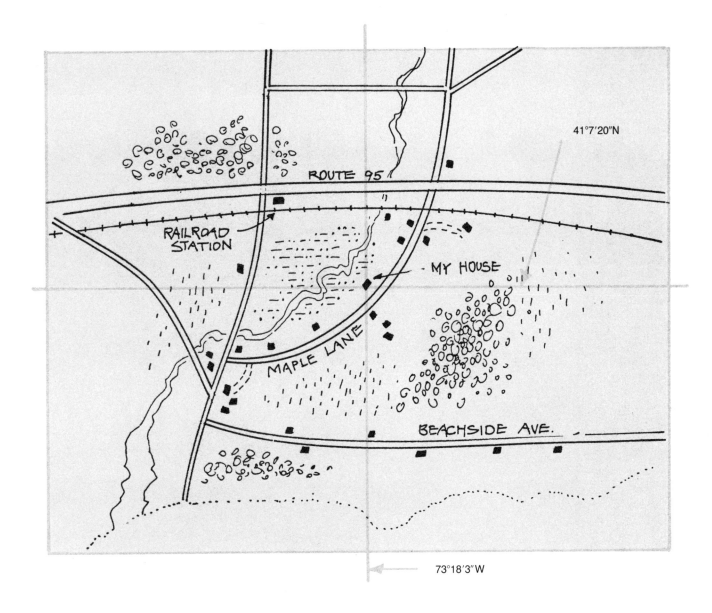

41°7'20"N

ROUTE 95

RAILROAD STATION

MY HOUSE

MAPLE LANE

BEACHSIDE AVE.

73°18'3"W

If you have the latitude and longitude of a place, all you need is an accurate, large-scale map to see just where it is.

The latitude of my house is 41 degrees, 7 minutes, and 20 seconds north of the equator. The proper way to write this is 41° 7′ 20″ N. Now we know how far above the equator my house is. However, we don't know how far east or west of the Greenwich meridian it is. But I have looked at a map and figured out that it is 73 degrees, 18 minutes, and 3 seconds west of the Greenwich meridian.

If you were the space traveler mentioned at the beginning of this book and you wanted to come visit me, you would need a large-scale map and this data: 41° 7′ 20″ N and 73° 18′ 3″ W. Then you could find where these lines of latitude and longitude crossed and land your spaceship right in my back yard!

If you and a friend understand about latitude and longitude, you can have some interesting conversation from time to time. You might say, "Well, why don't we meet for lunch at 50° 10′ N, 2° 40′ E?" (Your friend would have to do a bit of traveling to meet you there, however. Look it up on a map of the world and see where it is. The answer is at the bottom of page 40.)

6.

Until about five hundred years ago most people believed
the earth was flat. If it was a round ball, wouldn't everything
fall off the bottom side? They also worried about the edge of
the earth. If it was flat, wouldn't you tumble over the side if
you wandered off too far?

This was a very troublesome question, and it took an
adventurous sailor, Ferdinand Magellan, to prove that the
earth really was round. He sailed from Spain in 1519 heading
west, and he kept going for three years — always going west, west,
west — until his ship ended up back where it started from. The
earth was definitely round!

The only really accurate way to see what our round earth is like is to use a globe. Some lucky people own globes, and many schools and libraries have them. It is a fine way to locate places and see how they relate to one another. But a globe is not a very practical thing to carry when on a hike or traveling in a car. Besides, a globe can't show close-up views of anything unless it is enormously large. Much handier is a paper map that can be rolled up or folded.

In order to show the round surface of the earth on a piece of paper, some changes must be made. If you could cut off the "skin" of the earth and paste it down on a flat surface, you would get something like the map on the top of the opposite page. There would be big gaps at the top and bottom. If the top and bottom edges were stretched so that they came together, you would get a different-looking map — it would be like the one underneath it, where the gaps are filled in.

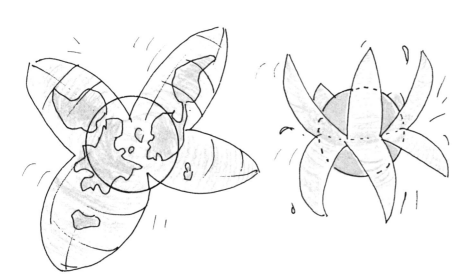

There are many other ways of "peeling" off the surface of the earth to produce different kinds of maps.

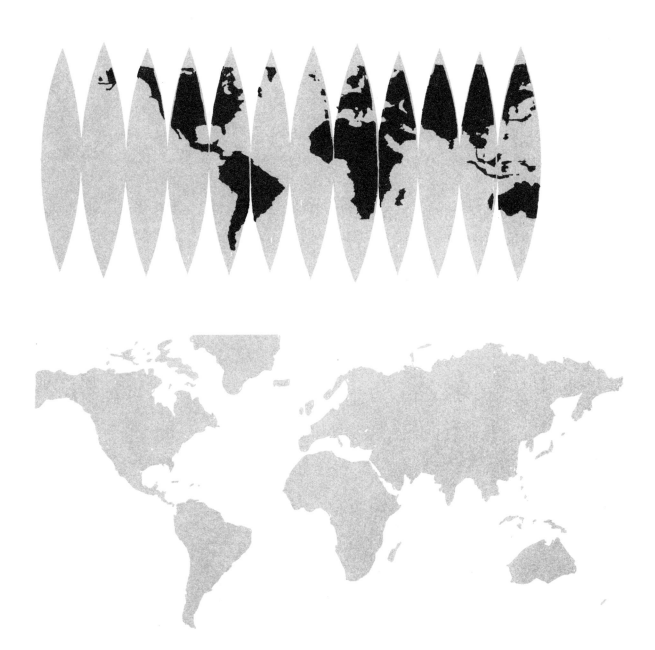

Because of the stretching of the top and bottom, some areas are distorted. They appear much bigger than they actually are. In the sixteenth century a geographer named Gerhardus Mercator developed a different kind of map, which is widely used today. Although there are distortions at the top and bottom, the Mercator Projection is accurate enough along the center.

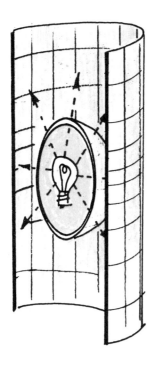

This is how a Mercator Projection is made:

Think of the earth as a hollow ball with a light inside it. When the light shines through the ball, its image will be projected onto the sheet of paper wrapped around it. All the lines of latitude and longitude will be parallel, but the lines of latitude on top and bottom will be farther apart.

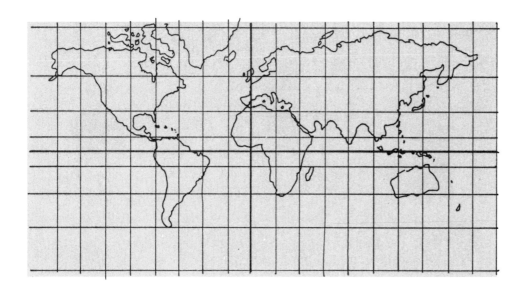

In the Mercator Projection, the lines of latitude spread farther apart as they move away from the equator.

On a large-scale map, the area covered is small, and the lines of latitude and longitude are nice and straight and even. But when you look at a map that covers a large part of the earth's surface, you'll see these lines usually curve or lean at rather odd angles! This is because of the mapmaker's efforts to draw the earth in various particular ways. Each way has its limitations as well as its advantages. For example, the Mercator Projection has the top and bottom out of proportion. Other maps, like Goode's Interrupted Projection, show the continents with accuracy, but there are other distortions that make for a rather peculiar-looking map.

Different kinds of maps are called projections because they *project* the round earth's surface onto a flat surface. As you can see, this is a complicated business. Mapmaking requires the skill and experience of highly trained experts and lots of complicated mathematics.

Many mapmakers have spent a great deal of thought trying to develop the one, all-purpose map that will be most useful for the most people. But there is no such thing as a perfect map that will suit *all* needs!

A map like this is called a Goode's Interrupted Projection and may look a little strange at first glance. But it shows the area of the continents with great accuracy and is very useful for that reason.

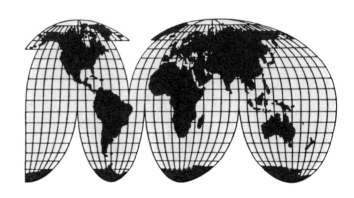

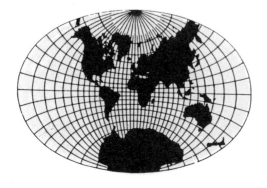

In this projection, Antarctica appears unusually large.

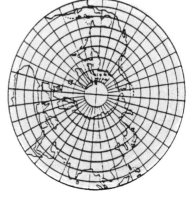

This is a polar projection showing the North Pole area.

7.
ON THE WATER

When a map is intended for use by people on boats, it is no longer called a map. It is called a chart, or a marine chart, and it is absolutely essential for safe traveling on water.

One of the reasons a chart is so important is that there is no way to tell what is under the water simply by looking. You can see an island, or something sticking up out of the water, but a smooth, flat stretch may look quite safe yet have all kinds of dangers just inches below the surface.

In some places the water might be very clear and you'd be able to see down a few feet. But this is not often the case, and if you were traveling fast and didn't have a chart, you wouldn't know if there was a sandbar, a reef, a big rock, or something else that you were about to crash into.

This part of a large marine chart shows an island (Block Island) and a stretch of the mainland at the top.

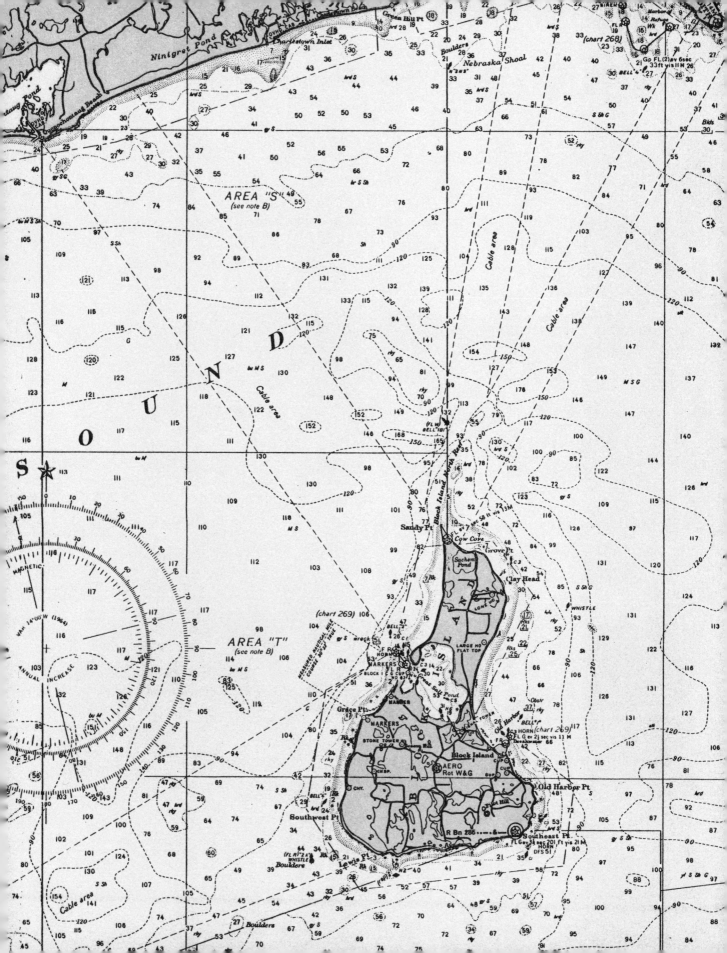

If a rowboat bumps into a hidden rock, there may be no more damage than a bit of paint scraped off the side or bottom. But what happens if a huge tanker filled with millions of gallons of oil runs onto a jagged reef? This sort of accident has caused terrible oil spills, damaging hundreds of miles of coastline and destroying much wildlife.

Marine charts show coastlines, harbors, lighthouses, buoys, and all the things that help a boat travel safely from one place to another. As well as indicating underwater dangers, a chart shows the depth of water everywhere. That is the purpose of the small numbers scattered around. If, for

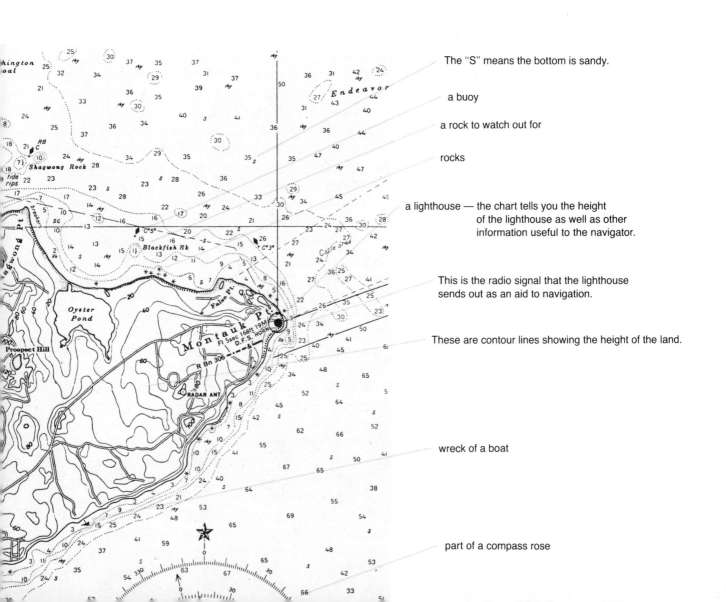

The "S" means the bottom is sandy.

a buoy

a rock to watch out for

rocks

a lighthouse — the chart tells you the height of the lighthouse as well as other information useful to the navigator.

This is the radio signal that the lighthouse sends out as an aid to navigation.

These are contour lines showing the height of the land.

wreck of a boat

part of a compass rose

example, you see the number 6, that means there is 6 feet of water at that particular spot.

If you are sailing a boat with a keel that extends 8 feet down into the water and you are approaching a big rock that is *6* feet below the surface, you are headed for trouble! As you can see, those numbers are very important indeed.

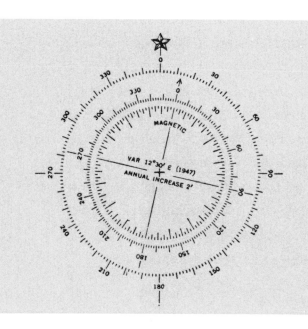

MARINE COMPASS ROSE

The outer circle, which is in degrees, shows true north. The inner circle, also showing degrees, points to magnetic north. (The compass, being magnetic, will point to magnetic north, not true north.) The difference between true north and magnetic north varies, depending on where you are located.

Like all maps, a marine chart has a compass rose. The compass rose shows both true north and magnetic north. This may sound complicated, and it is a bit of a nuisance, but it isn't as bad as it sounds. A compass will point to magnetic north. But — and this is a big "but" — true north, where the North Pole is located, is not the same place as magnetic north. All this means is that the navigator must decide whether to sail a true course or a magnetic course. This is an important matter if you are the navigator of a cargo ship sailing from San Francisco to Tokyo. But for people out in a small boat for an afternoon's fishing it is not worth worrying about, and magnetic readings, rather than true north readings, are usually used.

Marine charts come in different scales, just as regular land maps do. A large-scale chart (close-up view) will be what you want if you are just poking around near your home port. In a case like this it is not important to know water depths eighty miles away. On the other hand, if you are in a large ship crossing the Indian Ocean, you must have a small-scale chart that will give an all-over view of coastlines, islands, reefs, and have other information that might be needed for a safe passage.

The marine chart and the compass are the two basic tools for people who are out in boats. If you are out of sight of land and there is no landmark to head for, or if there is fog or bad weather, the compass plus the chart will tell you in what direction to steer if you want to get back to your home port or to any other destination. There are other, more technical navigation aids, such as radar and radio or satellite signals. These are mostly used on large ships. But the essential basics are chart and compass.

8.
SPECIAL-PURPOSE MAPS

There are all kinds of maps for many different purposes. There are weather maps in newspapers and on television. They tell us about cold fronts and high- and low-pressure areas and where you'll find snow or sun or rain.

There are maps that are made for airplane pilots, and ones for backpackers and for traveling by railroad. There are maps that explain the geology of a region, where forests are located, where certain crops are grown, and where energy sources of different kinds are located.

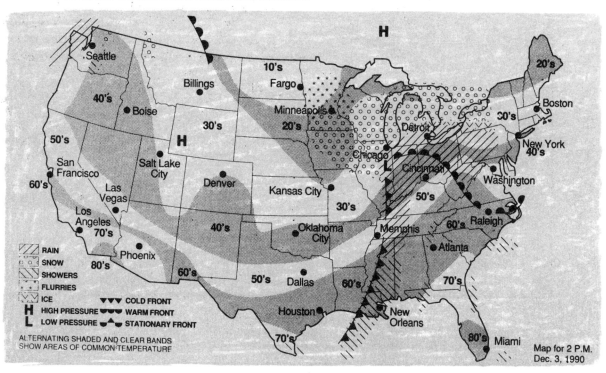

RAIN
SNOW
SHOWERS
FLURRIES
ICE
H HIGH PRESSURE
L LOW PRESSURE
▼▼▼ COLD FRONT
●●● WARM FRONT
▲▲ STATIONARY FRONT

ALTERNATING SHADED AND CLEAR BANDS
SHOW AREAS OF COMMON TEMPERATURE

Map for 2 P.M.
Dec. 3, 1990

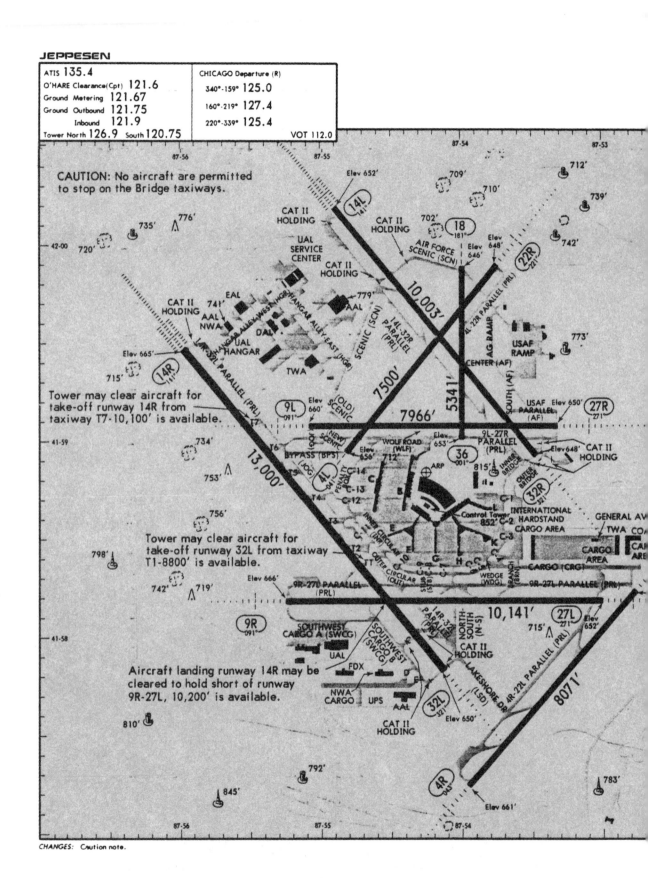

JEPPESEN

ATIS 135.4	CHICAGO Departure (R)
O'HARE Clearance(Cpt) 121.6	340°-159° 125.0
Ground Metering 121.67	160°-219° 127.4
Ground Outbound 121.75	220°-339° 125.4
Inbound 121.9	
Tower North 126.9 South 120.75	VOT 112.0

CAUTION: No aircraft are permitted
to stop on the Bridge taxiways.

CAT II HOLDING

14L

UAL SERVICE CENTER

CAT II HOLDING

AIR FORCE SCENIC (SCN)

18

22R

CAT II HOLDING

EAL 741'

AAL NWA

DAL

HANGAR ALLEY-WEST (HGR)

HANGAR ALLEY-EAST (HGR)

AAL 779'

SCENIC (SCN)

10,003'

USAF RAMP

773'

UAL HANGAR

TWA

14L-32R PARALLEL (PRL)

4L-22R RAMP

CENTER (AF)

SOUTH (AF)

USAF PARALLEL (AF)

Elev 665'

14R

Tower may clear aircraft for
take-off runway 14R from
taxiway T7-10,100' is available.

14R-32L PARALLEL (PRL)

9L

(OLD) SCENIC

7500'

5341'

7966'

9L-27R PARALLEL (PRL)

CAT II HOLDING

27R

(NEW) SCENIC

BYPASS (BPS)

WOLF ROAD (WLF)

712'

36

815'

INNER BRIDGE

OUTER BRIDGE

734'

13,000'

753'

PENALTY BOX

C-14

C-13

C-12

C

B

ARP

32R

INTERNATIONAL HARDSTAND

GENERAL AV

756'

INNER CIRCULAR (INR)

C-11

Control Tower 852'

C-2

CARGO AREA

TWA

Tower may clear aircraft for
take-off runway 32L from taxiway
T1-8800' is available.

OUTER CIRCULAR (OUT)

CARGO (CRG)

CARGO AREA

798'

Elev 666'

9R-27L PARALLEL (PRL)

WEDGE (WDG)

BRANCH (BRN)

9R-27L PARALLEL (PRL)

742' 719'

9R

SOUTHWEST CARGO A (SWCG)

SOUTHWEST CARGO B (SWCG)

10,141'

27L

14R-32L PARALLEL (PRL)

NORTH-SOUTH (N-S)

CAT II HOLDING

LAKESHORE DR (LSD)

4R-22L PARALLEL (PRL)

8071'

UAL

FDX

NWA CARGO

UPS

AAL

32L

Aircraft landing runway 14R may be
cleared to hold short of runway
9R-27L, 10,200' is available.

CAT II HOLDING

810'

792'

4R

845'

783'

Elev 661'

CHANGES: Caution note.

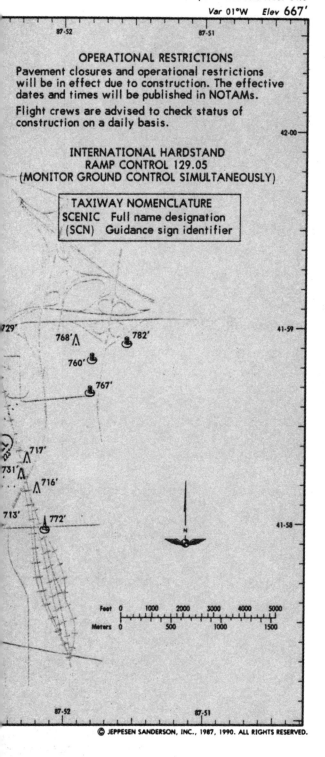

CHICAGO, ILL
-O'HARE INTL

ORD 113.9-On Airport   N41 58.8 W087 54.3

Var 01°W   Elev 667'

OPERATIONAL RESTRICTIONS

Pavement closures and operational restrictions
will be in effect due to construction. The effective
dates and times will be published in NOTAMs.

Flight crews are advised to check status of
construction on a daily basis.

**INTERNATIONAL HARDSTAND
RAMP CONTROL 129.05
(MONITOR GROUND CONTROL SIMULTANEOUSLY)**

TAXIWAY NOMENCLATURE
SCENIC   Full name designation
(SCN)   Guidance sign identifier

This is a map for airplane pilots. It shows the approaches to O'Hare International Airport in Chicago, Illinois. The directions and lengths of the various runways are clearly marked. The loading and storage and service areas are located. Even the surrounding roads and railroad tracks are shown, though only faintly. The heights of various buildings and towers are also indicated, so that low-flying aircraft will know where they are and be sure to avoid them. There is, in fact, an enormous amount of information contained on this one small map — which is reproduced here at actual size. Maps like this are absolutely essential if pilots are to make safe, comfortable, controlled landings.

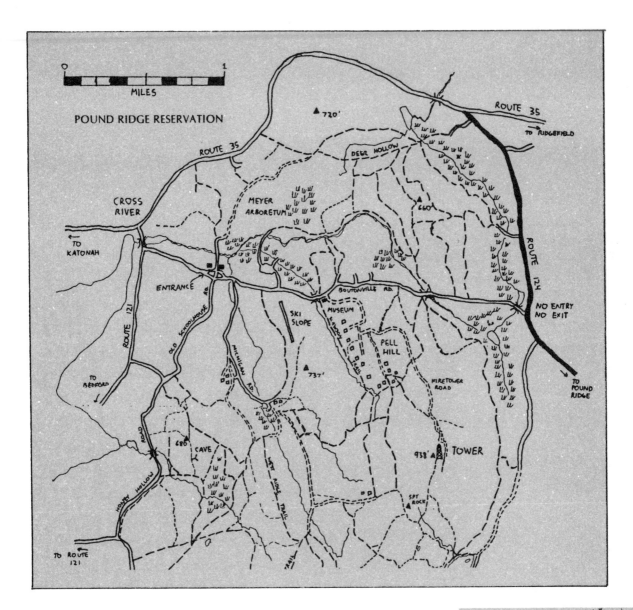

POUND RIDGE RESERVATION

Serious hikers will usually use the sort of topographic map shown on page 29. But for just a short afternoon hike through a state park, or a little bike expedition, or a walk along a nature trail, a simple map will usually be all you need. A map like the one above covers only a few square miles but is very useful. It shows roads, trails, and points of interest and would keep you from getting lost.

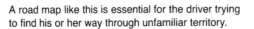
A road map like this is essential for the driver trying to find his or her way through unfamiliar territory.

A map is needed if you want to find your way in a strange city. And it is most certainly necessary for getting about in a complicated subway system like New York's. Without a map like the one here, it is pretty much impossible. Over the years mapmakers have tried many different ways to explain how, when, and where the trains go. The generous use of color, which is not shown here, is of much help. The section of map reproduced covers the various subway lines in Lower Manhattan.

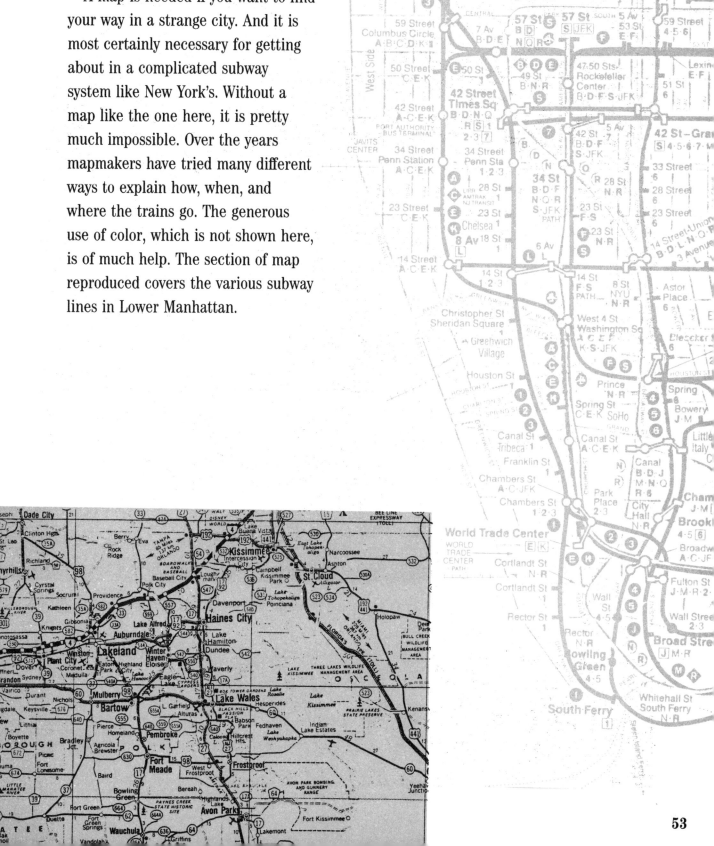

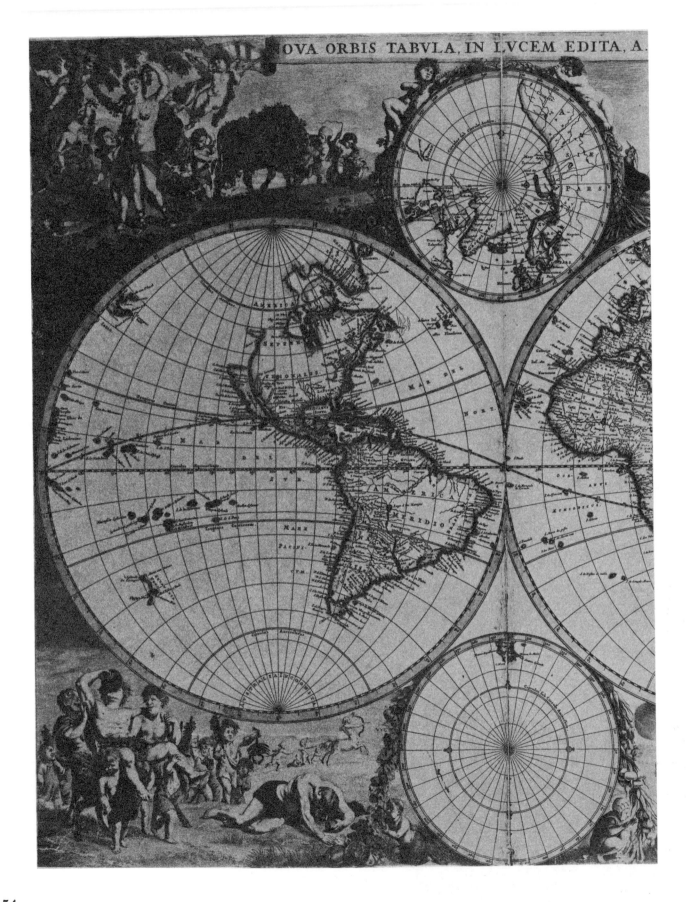

9.

HOW MAPS ARE MADE

Most ancient maps were based on drawings and reports by explorers and travelers to distant places. Mapmaking involved a lot of guesswork. When there was a blank space and the mapmaker didn't know what to do, he would draw whatever struck his fancy. Some early maps have sea monsters and angels and strange creatures scattered around them. Often quite elaborate scenes were tucked away in odd corners and left-over spaces outside the map itself, as in the one on the facing page. Many of these antique maps are quite beautiful and are much valued by museums and collectors.

This is part of a map of the world that was made in 1670. As you can see, the mapmaker was a little uncertain about much of North America. California seems to be an island in the Pacific, off the west coast of the United States, and Alaska isn't to be seen anywhere at all!

For many years fairly accurate maps were made by teams of surveyors. In 1804 Lewis and Clark, who were both surveyors and explorers, set off on a two-year trip across uncharted parts of America. The information they gathered prepared the way for many others. One important mapmaker who came along some forty years later was a government officer named Charles Frémont, who produced the map on these pages. It is one part of a set of maps that described the route

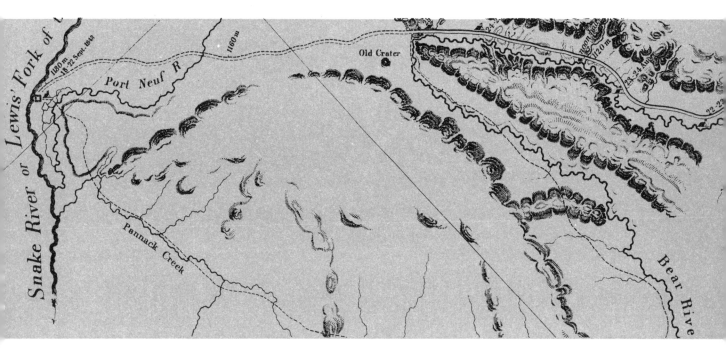

from the midwest, through the Rocky Mountains, all the way to the Pacific Ocean. These maps showed the way for the many adventurous settlers who traveled westward to find more and better farmland or who sometimes just wanted to head west and get away from what they considered crowded town life. The trail they followed, which is on this map, is called the Oregon Trail.

These maps also contained many notes describing what Frémont encountered along the way, and had much useful data about location of fuel, water, grass for horses and cattle. There were even warnings about hostile Indians. One of the maps has this to say: "Good guards ought to be kept all the way. Sioux Indians are not to be trusted."

The maps, showing mountains and rivers and forests, provided information for the hunters, trappers, and farmers who eventually settled there. It isn't hard to imagine these early travelers slowly moving westward through this strange

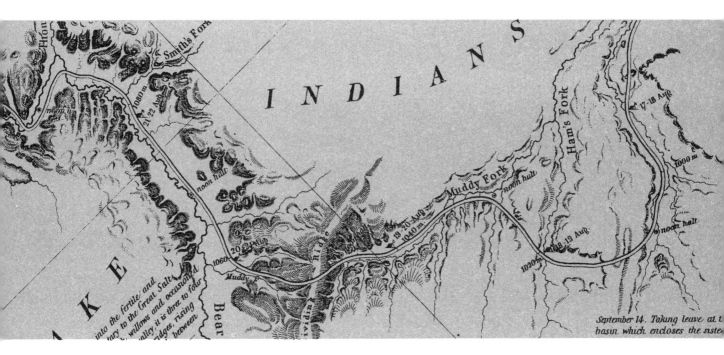

and unfamiliar territory, worrying about Indians, carrying all their possessions in heavy, lumbering wagons, with their children and relatives, their livestock, their horses. And these maps, so carefully compiled by Captain Frémont, were the one priceless, mile-by-mile guide. They were also the basis for roads and railway lines that were later built through these areas.

Lewis and Clark used compass readings and measurements to get the information they needed. By measuring distances and observing angles it is possible to work out a series of triangles that accurately describe an area. This method of measuring distances and angles is called triangulation. It is based on simple geometry, which says that you can compute the lengths of two sides of a triangle if you know the size of the third side and the angles made by the two adjoining sides. A system of triangles can be combined to cover a very large area.

A theodolite is a tool used by surveyors and mapmakers. It can measure vertical and horizontal angles with great accuracy.

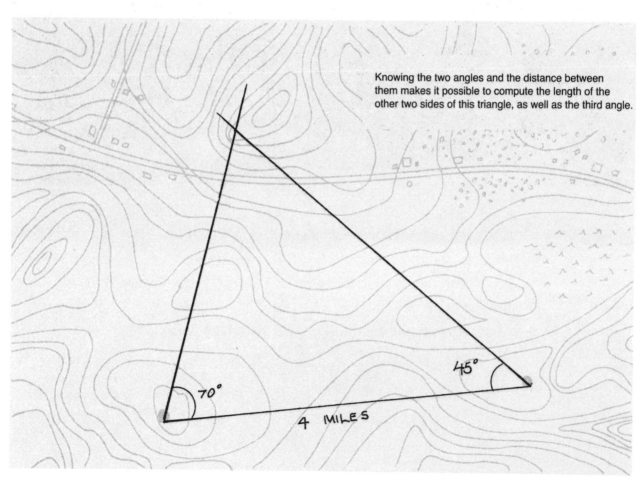

Knowing the two angles and the distance between them makes it possible to compute the length of the other two sides of this triangle, as well as the third angle.

70°

45°

4 MILES

Some fifty years ago aerial photography became a tool for mapmaking. Special cameras and drawing methods were used to make maps of areas that were difficult to reach on foot. This procedure has been used in countries all over the world. But even more precise mapmaking methods have been developed in the last few years by using satellites.

Satellites not only help mapmakers, but enable travelers to find their exact location anywhere on the earth. Let's say you are hiking in the wilderness or sailing in the middle of the ocean at night in heavy fog. If you have the right "sat-nav" equipment, you can press a button and a readout of your latitude and longitude will appear — accurate to within a few feet!

10.

MAKING YOUR OWN MAP

Making a really precise map that covers a large area is a job for an expert. But making a simple map of a small area — like your back yard, or part of a park, or a section of the neighborhood where you live — is not too difficult an undertaking. It is fun to do and will teach you some of the basic methods of mapmaking.

You will need these tools: A large sheet of paper about sixteen inches square, a pencil with an eraser, a protractor (this is a semicircular device used to measure angles), and, most important, a compass. A prismatic compass like the one shown lets you sight an object and at the same time read its bearing. But a plain compass will also do the job, though it won't be as accurate.

This is a prismatic compass with sighting vanes. It has no needle. The entire face of the compass turns to show north.

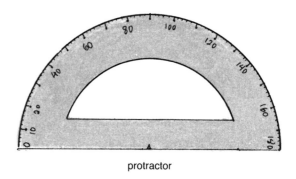

protractor

This is an inexpensive, common variety of compass. It has a needle which points north. (You must use a compass that shows degrees.)

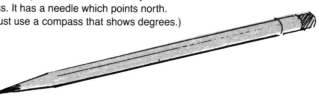

Here's how to do it:

1. Choose a spot in the middle of the area you want to map. Mark it with a wooden stake or a rock. This is the center point from which you will make all your measurements. Mark this spot in the center of your paper.

2. Stand next to the stake or rock that marks your center point. With your compass find out which way is north. Draw a line from the center point to show it.

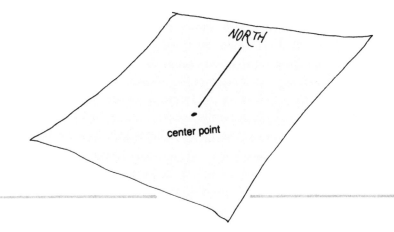

3. Pick a conspicuous object not too far away, such as a tree or a corner of a building. Let's assume it is a tree. Take a bearing by sighting over the compass and reading how many degrees from north the compass shows.

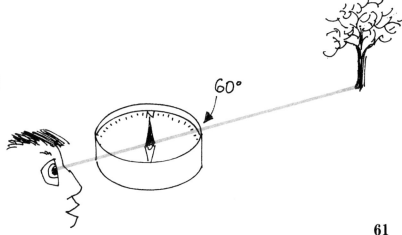

4. Place the protractor over the center point on your paper and mark the angle of the bearing with a pencil line.

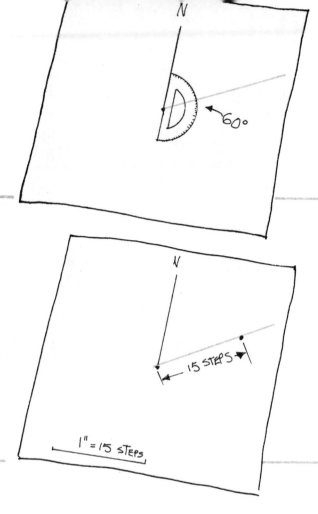

5. Now you know the *direction* of the tree. But if the map is to be of any use, you must know how far away the tree is. If you have a very long tape measure, you can use that. Or you can use a yardstick and flip it over and over to get your distance. Another easy way is to pace off the distance, using "steps" as a measure of distance instead of feet or yards.

Once you have measured or paced off the distance, you must decide on a scale so that you can show this distance on your map. You may decide a convenient scale is 1 inch equals 4 steps, or 1 inch equals 6 steps, or whatever you find fits best. (If you are unsure about this business of scale, reread pages 17 and 18.) Finally, make a dot on the bearing line at the distance you have measured. You now have the direction and distance of the tree.

6. Use this same method for all the other objects you want to include on your map. With buildings you won't be able to get bearings on more than two or three corners. So you will have to figure out the shape of a building by walking around it and perhaps doing some special measuring.

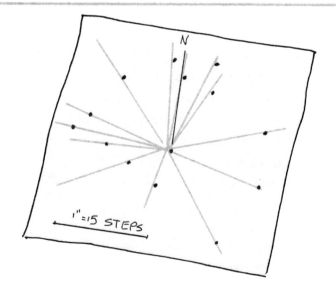

Most protractors show only 0 to 180 degrees. (This is half of 360 degrees, which is a complete circle.) In this case, when you get a compass bearing that is more than 180 degrees, you will have to do a little subtraction. Let's suppose you got a compass bearing of 300 degrees on something. Subtract 180 from 300 and you get 120. Place your protractor so that 180 is at the top (pointing north) and read off 120 degrees. This will actually be your 300-degree bearing. Sound complicated? Try it once and you'll see it isn't as tricky as it sounds. Of course, if you have the kind of round protractor that shows 360 degrees, you won't have to bother with all this.

7. After you have taken all your bearings and measured your distances, you will have a lot of lines and dots on your paper. Connect the dots that represent buildings or roads. Sketch in trees or streams or whatever else you have included. Then erase your bearing lines, and you will have your map!

The final step to make your map neat and attractive is to carefully label whatever you think is important. Then you might want to add a compass rose, some color, or a ruled border. Don't forget to show the scale of your map.

11.
MORE ABOUT MAPS

An atlas is a collection of maps and map information in book form. It is a very useful thing to have. A good atlas is not inexpensive and should be chosen carefully. There are different kinds. You might want an atlas of road maps, or one of just the United States, or one that will contain all the countries in the world (this would be called a world atlas). Some atlases will also show land forms, population, and pollution, and contain much other specialized information.

Individual maps for hiking and backpacking (called topographic maps) can often be purchased in stores that sell camping and outdoor activity supplies. These maps can also be purchased from the Department of the Interior, Geological Survey, Reston, Virginia 22092. If you send a letter asking about maps for the area you are interested in, you will get information on how you can order by mail. (This is a rather slow process, however.) They will also tell you which government offices have maps to sell. In some large cities you may find stores that sell maps. Marine charts are sold in boating supply stores.

A very useful and informative book that will tell you in great detail where and how you can obtain maps is *The Map Catalog: Every Kind of Map and Chart on Earth and Even Some Above It,* Joel Makower, editor, published by Vintage Books.